Paige
the
Panda Bear

Paige the Panda Bear

©2023 Jenny Schreiber

In Association with:
Elite Online Publishing
63 East 11400 South
Suite #230
Sandy, UT 84070
EliteOnlinePublishing.com

ISBN: *978-1-956642-72-8 (Paperback)*
ISBN: *978-1-956642-73-5 (Hardback)*

Paige the Panda Bear

by Jenny Schreiber

Meet Paige
the panda bear.

Panda bears are black and white.

Paige has
large black circles
around her eyes.

Paige is a very
good climber.

Paige is
a very good
swimmer.

Paige eats
bamboo plants.

Paige has very sharp teeth to crush bamboo.

Paige the panda bear
is native to China.

Paige is a very peaceful animal.

Paige is a very social bear and lives in a group called a clan.

Paige is very playful and loves to roll around with other panda bears.

Paige is very smart
and uses tools
to find food.

Paige uses smell to find food and avoid danger.

Paige is very good at
sleeping for
a long time.

Paige is an endangered species. There are only a few thousand left in the world.

Paige plays a vital role in maintaining the balance of the forest.

Paige is loved by
people all over
the world.

Paige is a symbol of peace and harmony on earth.

PEACE ON EARTH

The End

Find More books by Jenny Schreiber

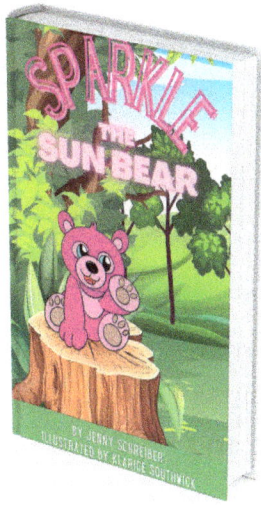

SPARKLE THE SUN BEAR
BY JENNY SCHREIBER
ILLUSTRATED BY KLARICE SOUTHWICK

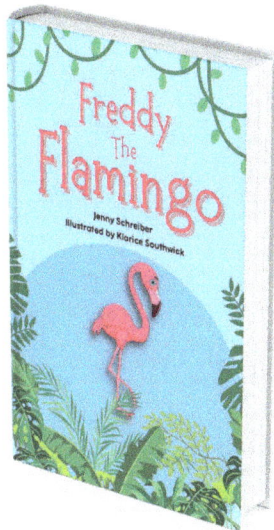

Freddy The Flamingo
Jenny Schreiber
Illustrated by Klarice Southwick

PIPER THE POLAR BEAR
JENNY SCHREIBER

CHESTER THE FUZZY CHIPMUNK
JENNY SCHREIBER

Animal Facts Children's Book Series

Paige the
Panda Bear

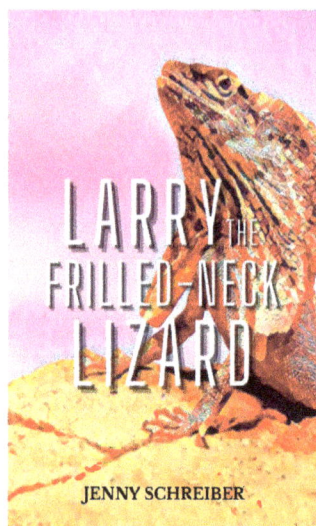

Larry the
Frilled-Neck Lizard

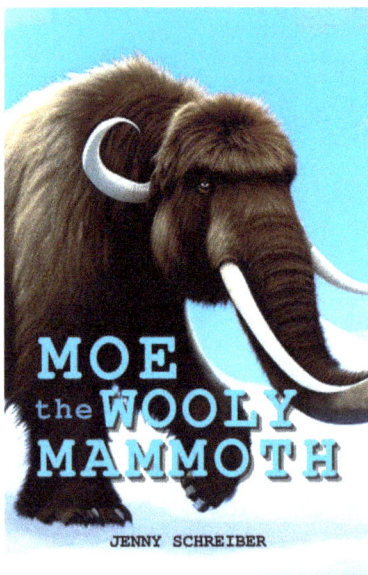

Moe the Wooly
Mammoth

www.ingramcontent.com/pod-product-compliance
Lightning Source LLC
Chambersburg PA
CBHW052124030426
42335CB00025B/3104